The Beginning of Undoing

The Beginning of Undoing

Poems by

John Milkereit

© 2025 John Milkereit. All rights reserved.
This material may not be reproduced in any form, published,
reprinted, recorded, performed, broadcast,
rewritten or redistributed without
the explicit permission of John Milkereit.
All such actions are strictly prohibited by law.

Cover design by Shay Culligan
Cover image by Kelly Penrod
Author photo by John Milkereit

ISBN: 978-1-63980-847-2

Kelsay Books
502 South 1040 East, A-119
American Fork, Utah 84003
Kelsaybooks.com

*What we call the beginning is often the end.
And to make an end is to make a beginning.
The end is where we start from.*

~T.S. Eliot

Acknowledgments

I am incredibly appreciative of poets Cait Weiss Orcutt and David Meischen, who reviewed this collection and made insightful comments. They have facilitated poetry classes where I generated several poems in this collection.

Also, I am fortunate to belong to two writing critique groups. One is Poets in the Loop, where many of these poems were workshopped initially. Thank you, Mary, Elina, Dom, Winston, Chuck, Kelly, Vanessa, Carrie, and Varsha. San Miguel Poetry participants also critiqued these poems and made them better. Athena Saenz formatted the final touches of all the pages and photos.

Additionally, I hired my trusted editor (ever since my MFA days), Chelsey Clammer, who ultimately waved her wand for editorial magic to appear.

Finally, thank you to the following publications, in which versions of these poems previously appeared, sometimes under different titles:

Abandoned Mine: "Cooking Class," "A Prayer," "Against Isolation"
The Comstock Review: "Pisces: Triplex"
The Ekphrastic Review: "I Will Talk Peace," "Born to Be Wild," "Prayer Is a Vast Country," "The Alien Said *Yes*," "It's Come to This," "When the Whole World Wears a Costume," "You Can't Always Get What You Want," "Aubade with Circle Game," "Upon Seeing the Glorious Crepuscular Rays," "Invitation"
Equinox: "What We Found in Space," "The Hyde Park Babysitter," "Shelter," "Cento: What Kind of Quagmire Is This?"
How to Tend a Wall: Friendswood Library Ekphrastic Poetry Anthology (Friends of the Friendswood Library): "Born to Be Wild," "Pissarro"

Kitchen Sink Magazine: "Bowen's Island Restaurant"
Panoply: "When the Whole World Is Short-Staffed," "Pasture"
Synkroniciti: "Newspaper Photograph of Border Agents Discussing the Separation of a Family," "License Renewal"
Unknotting The Line: The Poetry in Prose (Dos Gatos Press): "Reunion"

Contents

The Road I Built for Memory	13
A Prayer	15
Against Isolation	16
A Pool of Yellow Glow	17
You Can't Always Get What You Want	19
Watching My Father	20
All You Need Is Love	21
What We Found in Space	22
The Model Railroad	23
The Hyde Park Babysitter	25
Pisces: Triplex	26
Lake Shore Drive	27
Nostalgia, 1970s	30
How to Stay Healthy	31
Pissarro	33
The Trick to Caring for a Cat Named *Mardi Gras*	34
Of Blur	35
Bowen's Island Restaurant	36
The Alien Said *Yes*	37
It's Come to This	39
I Tried to Write a Memoir Called *Low Country Debacle;* I Failed	40
When I Dial Up the Elements of a Reggae, Rock, and Punk Band	42
When the Whole World Wears a Costume	46

*

When Molecules Shed at the Driveway Movie Party	49
See Silver	50
Still-Life with Three Musicians and a Dog	52

Shelter	53
When Life Calmly Gives Out Its Secret	54
The Quiet Undoing	55
Newspaper Photograph of Border Agents Discussing the Separation of a Family	56
Upon Seeing the Glorious Crepuscular Rays	58
I Will Talk Peace	60
License Renewal	62
Reunion	64
Letter to Lincoln Fox	65
The Whole World Is a Work of Art	66
Climbing Up to *Tres Cruces,* San Miguel de Allende	70
Cooking Class	71
Comfort	72
Invitation	73

*

Born to Be Wild	77
Blood & Air	78
When Are We Arriving?	79
Driving to Dallas on Good Friday for My Brother's Oyster Roast	80
Cento: What Kind of Quagmire Is This?	82
Home Run	84
Pasture	85
Epiphany	86
Aging Disgracefully	87
Shocking Love Poem	88
If Life Is So Much More Evaluating Than It Appears, Why Isn't There a Hotline to Call?	89

The Dodo	90
One Night I Pretended the World Didn't Exist	91
What Gentles Skin But Isn't	92
Aubade with Circle Game	93
Willy Wonka	95
When the Whole World Is Short-Staffed	97
Notes	99

The Road I Built for Memory

For the rest area, tiny moths will flutter like scraps of paper.

Bricks will be repurposed from a hurricane wall into a walkway

that leads to plush bathrooms with endless mirrors, water,
    and soap.

Vending machines will be stocked with seed packets of words.

This is a road for plenty of reflection, triggered by staring at
    the water after a troubling rain.

This road has an exit for a spare jalopy in case memory breaks
    down.

This is a road where blind-date locations appear as dropped
    pins on apps.

Emoji women wear sailor outfits; men wear navy-officer uniforms.
    We can press another button for a Disney+ face.

This is a road open during winter.

This is a road that tolerates cigarettes.

Roadside diners will serve thinking food—chocolate milk
    and spaghetti. They'll open shutters to clouds—paler
    and thinner ones than over the gulf.

This is not a climate-controlled road.

This road has laundry machines that clean clothes as white
   as snow.

This is a road almost to Gretna, almost to thrift stores, but a ferry
   is involved.

Let there be a road to New Orleans despite the zombie man on the
   Crescent train shouting, "Always keep your pants zipped!"

This is a road for superglue.

This is a road for elephants to march off to the circus.

Jesus loves this road because it converges on the Lucky Dog
   Casino.

This is a road for wooden stakes.

A road prettier and bigger than moth wings, but I'll still let them
   flutter at the rest stops all the same.

A Prayer

It seems to me that my parents saved a prayer,
pressing dreams for me flat as goldenrods in a book,
hoping they weren't bringing up extraterrestrials,
me first, then my brothers. We hovered over
our experiments: one, a gerbil who escaped inside
the planet of a radiator; another, a rock tumbler
polishing stones to practice our first steps on the moon.
We trained in the basement in the eclipse of
their watching, our bodies orbiting the ping-pong table,
astronauts unaware we were approaching a six-pointed
violet star, the celestial lily, parents turned to pale blue dots.

Against Isolation

If I could take back that clear night
when I assumed love in a movie theater
could rescue me from a dull Code Red,
would the tall pine trees still have stood
watching off Strawberry Lane? If I
could take you in your faux sailor suit
& slight tan on a sailboat ride,
ditching my new white Honda
purchased at the dealership from Stan,
who set us up blind, we would've gone
to the lake, and untied a ride from a dock,
rope from the cleats. If I could take
your hunger, because you'd like to fork
catfish, we'd eat at Murrell's,
then navigate to the glass factory.
The way your fingers would touch the skinny
legs of overstocked champagne flutes
as if they were tiny rescue animals you'd
want, and how I would've fed you, "Yes,
absolutelys." Back then, I was 24, living in
Shreveport, barely getting into the economy,
buying packs of cigarettes for my neighbor if
she agreed to cook before we watched
Murder, She Wrote. My TV tray whispered
I could have every ash-laden seat
float away, dark buoys, too many raggedy
edges that clung. I didn't know then how
quick the credits come.

A Pool of Yellow Glow

Applesauce stirred warm
      with cinnamon stick.
           Bowls, little wolf moons

set on blue-and-green placemats.
      Plastic—easy for
           wiping away spills.

Grandmother taught my brothers and me
      Yahtzee. Shake dice, cup
           hands, hope the dots

land where we wanted. Cube-shaped
      happiness. Ruby rush! "Oh, that's nice,"
           we repeated her after a good roll.

Supper was an apple
      without a core, a dumpling
           baked and wrapped in pie dough.

After our bedtime, grown-ups played Pinochle.
      Murmured voices, laughter, the faint smell
           of burnt tobacco,

smoke like dialogue clouds
      from our comic books. We spied ankles
           by peeking under the door.

Loneliness was a pool
      of yellow glow. I just wanted
           a chair at the table to watch.

Bored the next morning, we found a hammer,
    smashed Black Label beer caps,
        coated undersides still hops-scented.

We flattened enough to rattle in Sucrets tins.
    She drove us downtown to the Five & Dime
        for baseball cards and marbles.

The electric apples—their aluminum foil
    wrappings—we inserted them into wall sockets.
        Jolted for joy, we lifted.

You Can't Always Get What You Want

But you could talk to the blue-shadowed
tablecloth, its red lamps bathing
the evening glow. You could try to touch
the woman's arm, winglike,
who is fatally attracted to fire. You could
offer to pour her wine left in the bottle—
hopefully, not the passed-over sips of Spain.
It's July 1970. The gaze and graceful contours
of a coterie. The glaze of look-up smiles
and look-back glances. You could dilate your eyes
and not be escorted. Could find love, if not here,
then as an embrace, gusts of awareness. Sing and pray.
See towards heaven past the unfinished cathedral.
You can't choose who sits at the table; her chair
was the last available, or maybe you blundered
in later. You can't expect a teapot to pour, so pour it.
Can't expect the sugar cubes to plop in the cup,
so plop. The cigarette is a lousy chimney. And if
it's troubling that more decades rumble by, you
can still remember the dark brown fur of a moose
roaming the thin, forest floor on an island in boyhood,
and chocolate chips snuck from a yellow, crinkly bag
when your mother wasn't looking. That rock-and-roll
song is burned into your skin, like your father's voice,
the semisweet advice that won't come for another fifty
years. You get what you need. The woman stares
until she turns to you, her face aglow.
She says: *You wouldn't understand.*
But you do, & then she flies away.

Watching My Father

Not a bat,
more like a giant raven,
pale face splashed in Old Spice.
The mirror behind the basket
of trick-or-treat apples
reflects his starkness.
The dark cape presses midnight
against the hallway wall.
He schemes how to unveil
his cosmos. The cape
cuts along the staircase
chasing screams
past the glass door,
then the front door leading
to the private park.
His hair is a slick mountain.
His mustache says no bird.
His jawbone is a sculpture.
I am ten and laughing
out my guts.

All You Need Is Love

that's fair, make love not war, falling head over heels.

Life is the flower—love is the honey; call it madness,

it's called love, learn to love by loving, in the love tunnel,

love thy neighbor, Bob Love dribbling a basketball, love

makes the world go round, love is blind, the love of life,

face only a mother could . . . puppy loveable, love that dog,

love warts and all, love—hate relationship, Queen's "Crazy Little

Thing Called Love," a life lived in love is never dull,

Bette Midler bellowed, "Love Me with a Feeling," probably

endlessly, *Love in the Time of Cholera* and *Serial Killers,*

Love in the Dark, Love on the Brain—a story about a

neuroscientist asking what Marie Curie would do,

Love Me Do, Do It for Love, love stamp by Robert Indiana,

and now, thank God, stamped *Forever,* love is the lovebird child,

love is the answer in bed; true love stories never have endings.

I'd love to.

What We Found in Space

Boys & girls always kiss in bushes. They climb trees.
I murmured this during Hide & Seek.

And in that moment, as we bordered
my grandmother's backyard, our pursed lips

like yellow star-grass petals pressed forward.
Sparkles touched inside my planet head.

O how leaving is. Pine-scented palms.
You clasped my hand anyway. Our flight path

zooming past the squirrel sentries in your driveway,
past your hidden parents, onto upstairs, and the capsule

of your bedroom. I didn't know we had lifted
off to play another game, one beginning

when a spaceship lands on the surface
of a comforter. How I wanted you not

to declare *I've already kissed another boy
seventeen times.* How I didn't expect

your voice might flash, fast as a comet, to crater
my *not-kissing-anyone-before* subsurface.

But there I was. A doll now dressed up
as a breathless astronaut, helmet punctured,

oxygen softly hissing from tubes previously
unknown in the underworld of us.

The Model Railroad

It was a Christmas present,
a one of a kind that lifted
and closed into the wall

like an ironing board.
It was made four-by-eight-foot
with plywood and space

underneath to run wiring for the train.
Cork was glued on the backside
to tack posters of rock bands or news articles.

Unfolded, I could touch
the branches of dead, sea-foamed green trees,
the creamed roof of a café.

It had no urge to pursue a location,
pleased to live in this bedroom
and display night during a winter morning

or to vanish during school hours
folded vertically in its own
darkness, the Esso gas station

with a bronze car suspended,
the attendant oblivious to gravity
as he continued to pump gasoline.

What a fright for a hamster
who escaped his cage,
dirty behind the radiator,

if he heard the hum of a locomotive
crossing a grating or saw park lamps
smaller than himself.

Once, I dropped him off in town.
The train never stopped except when
rocks from the gravel car emptied,

later scooped up with a spatula.
The people on the front porch
didn't seem bothered by his leg

covering Main Street or his tail
draped over the power lines.
The power never went out.

They weren't bothered by The Police singing
"Roxanne" on cassette either,
a song inspired by prostitutes in Paris

and a character from the play, *Cyrano de Bergerac*.
They had never been to France or seen
a play, and neither had their operator, not yet

since memory hasn't arrived.

The Hyde Park Babysitter

Marcus, the medical student, babysat us when my brothers & I lived in a condo. I don't know how he slotted time for us, biking in his dark blue scrubs, stethoscope circling his neck. Yet, there he'd be on a Friday night, face half-shaven, plopping his wrinkly, clothed self on the sofa, ready to watch Cher with us on TV. After fish sticks, we knew what he needed. A galaxy of Cheerios orbiting milk. He was like a zoo animal we weren't supposed to feed, who skipped breakfast until he could eat for free. He was our entertainer for a live show we didn't pay for, who wouldn't launch into burping lyrics until we tucked ourselves into bed. Crude melodies Cher couldn't cover. A disruption of fantasy, dreaming of Cher's hair cascading into our faces, a magical sheen, a fringe cut caressing our pajamas. After we left Chicago, we never saw Marcus again. I remember he said he loved her after a deep screen gaze the night she unraveled a pink pom-pom, revealing a contoured waist with a gateway navel. Later in life, Marcus became a hotshot doctor. I bet he met her backstage somewhere, finishing his cereal at home before their rendezvous.

Pisces: Triplex

Living authentically is a type of escape.
Honesty is the deepest stream.
Our bodies won't wash ashore for days.

       Assured, we wanted to plunge into each other.
       Blind from silt. Intuition:
       radar to help us see.

Intuition: our light-blue eyes can kiss stars.
A male fish in love will swim to
where she is waiting, or not.

       She is not in wait, wearing bright scales.
       Resin from the river is a grey gown
       searching for a matching veil.

If the search for love is too veiled, pull on hope.
Reel for dreams in the current.
She saw him drawn in black. He saw her as emerald waves.

       The black and emerald water
       drowns out dusk. Two fish swimming toward each other;
       escape is the opposite direction.

Lake Shore Drive

That was the year my clock radio
played The Eagles' "Take It to the Limit,"
on and on, the song echoing
during the family bike trek
to Buckingham Fountain.

We stopped at a playground
to ride the slide coiled like a snake,
to test if my stomach would lurch
on a seesaw. I pedaled
against the wind in all-star sneakers.
My spaceship called *Resistance*.

How could the smell of dead fish
have floated up this far?
A chain-link fence tine ambushed
the path, gouging one inch of my shin
like a rebel, not a gentle dandelion
rising from the grass. My awkward dismount,
motion in low gear. I wanted stars as guides.
Boat sails now dark matter. Gravity, a rope
across the skyline.

What would Sue, the dinosaur, have growled
in the museum we just passed?
With no allowance for an ice-cream sandwich,
I sat on the fountain's pink marble ledge.
My fingers reaching the water's bottom for a penny.

My wish was to trade my bicycle
for a bronze seahorse. If only I could have
a few limited rides under the blurred moonlight.
Then hold on and ask for a deep dive.

Prayer Is a Vast Country

and today, I'm the child kneeling, arms crossed.
Tomorrow, my pleas will zigzag.
On the third day, baby teeth will bite into my back.
My sorrow whips into a Roman tragedy:
angel eyes hand masked from bloody scars.
Right now, though,
I pray my witness
won't escape its remembrance.
In tragedy, praying hopes
to undo sins.
Pillars of prayer to hold onto.
Someday, I will grow up, pendulum
swinging pure innocence for new borders.
Will the cherubs fly over?
Sorry, I say to my prayer,
if I forget to pack you for travel.
I cannot dress you in a white robe.
Cherished, grey-winged, gardened,
spirited, honeymooned,
of all my coveted friends, only you, prayer,
gaze upon this stoned floor to endure.
Only you can bite the apple.

Nostalgia, 1970s

We felt desperate, entering a grocery store to cup our palms for snack mix from a bulk bin, first looking to see if anyone would care. No one did, so we proceeded to the bins, stomachs growling, hoping the lever would pull down without gaffes ~We felt desperate for miles, trudging to the post office to collect blocks of stamps to insert into an album, but wait a minute, we were there minutes ago, our gloves carrying the new found jewels, remembering the soldiers, and learning, framed in a city where *learning never ends* burning into the red and orange glow ~We felt desperate after licking fifteen cents' worth on an envelope, rushed a letter to the post office, scissored a stamp square off an envelope, stored in a stolen church pledge envelope, pencil stenciled like terrible graffiti & other stamps, *organized labor, proud & free,* with an eagle-etched background in a dusty album sitting on closet floor laminate laid down after the carpet dampened from leaky attic pipes ~Now that's desperation. The stamp album was payment for modeling children's clothes at Marshall Field's, back when it was called Marshall Field's, catalog pages we flipped on a golden retriever-slept-on sofa to carve our Christmas wish lists. Pushing our mothers one floor up on the escalator to purchase the largest box of Frango mints, since, guess why? Our pursed lips knew nothing joyful lasted long enough like roller coaster rides after stopping at a farm to purchase a yellow-winged butterfly ornament, novel to clip on a tree branch, and the anxiety followed by the anxiety while waiting for roller coaster rides and shooting ducks and missing ducks and flinging rings on Coke bottles for stuffed tigers even though we never won any tigers. Small loss is the shadow of riffraff, the dirty debris of riffraff.

How to Stay Healthy

Bake pizza in pie pans—first, make dough.
One catch: those yeast packets
will be impossible to find, camouflaged
in a grocery store aisle to test your eyes.
If you can't locate the fuel, you'll need
a formula, here called a "prescription."
Whatever you can or cannot find,
you fragile, gorgeous pilgrim, comfort
yourself by running around trying to look
proper. When my mother conducted
a cooking class, I showed up giddy
that I didn't have to use my hands.
The sizable overhead mirror inverted hers.
I relaxed in the back until it was over.
Then she wrote a cookbook with a famous
runner and titled the recipe, *Roadrunner Pizza*.
So, yes, you'll need to run. Measure your feet.
Buy shoes with memory foam. Run
to press the streets. Touch the gritty resin
at the school track. Try Lake Shore Drive,
and by this, I mean test your wind resistance.
The gym will offer a coach.
Someone to drill you on how to stretch.
The sweat, a new scent, will gently roll
off your forehead, salting your nights.
Each day, we tempt ourselves with junk.
There is no recipe to follow, just time trials
of reaching the silty bottom of our body
to smooth out the soul. So split a poblano pepper
and slice a white onion. Pluck cilantro and basil leaves.

Grease pans with a paper towel. Press dough
until firm enough to handle. The rest of the steps
are stories you've heard before. You will need a knife.
This is another way to cut yourself open.

Pissarro

He washes over me as a painting washes over a teenager,
as night hushes the dark voids of living.

Why would I avoid dancing in the city lights?
Why would I erase what I love as

a carriage, a street, a lamp, a café?
I've painted a few ugly canvases in *plein air.*

I've spied down from a hotel window overlooking
a river with silvery bulbs strung in bald cypresses.

My friends, I've never been to Paris.
The naked truth is the greys and blues.

The cold truth is ghosts remain, recessed
inside this interior. What infects your eye,

forms your view. What brush-stroked boldness
has you reborn from texture, its layered world?

The Trick to Caring for a Cat Named *Mardi Gras*

and coexisting inside a house
is proper spacing. Strung-

together nights, watching movies from Redbox,
resulted in her staring. The beginning of

undoing slipped out the front door when I
walked, escaping without my sensing her escape.

I didn't know the vet who called weeks later,
with news, then the inevitable

enjambment where I was king
of a parade float called *Guilt,* beads clinging

on a long-gone party, punctuation
flung on trees.

Of Blur

of a friend's disappearance,
of the bladder-bust bar game,

of class withdrawn from—
Mechanics of Deformable Bodies—
of seeing a boa constrictor squirming out of a backpack
while failing a midterm exam,

of the grand slam home-run ball almost caught,
of fake fraternity pledging,
of convincing sorority sisters that *football* is the wrong name,

of presence at the Indigo Girls concert in Little Five Points
before being cool, the guitar licks of loss, of France
and French-love disconnect,

of swim strokes and illegal climbing of Stone Mountain,
of a park patrol boat speeding, of bodies that could drown,
    "not washing ashore for five days,"

of not caring or fragility or found,
of bright obsessiveness,
of barely seeing Haley's Comet
    or was that the tail or where to drive?

of wrong way, of graduation into the abyss
    or pretending to walk into moon craters

of southern, not comfortable, the first trip near the old gold mines
of Helen, Georgia, sipped over ice.

Bowen's Island Restaurant

Sun-bleached shells outside,
a porch piecemealed, a tacked-on dock
like a tentacle. The front door, an ancient
secret.

The oyster room is oblong, cinder-blocked,
packed with old boxes and appliance parts
in mildew shadow.

Newspaper pages scatter as a tablecloth.
Cocktail sauce in a Pepsi bottle, a plain box
of opened saltine sleeves slumping
on a rickety table with mismatched chairs.
A snow shovel pitches bivalves into a fireplace.

Knives thrown down. No gloves. Cuts
inevitable from the muddy, sharp shells
you try to unhinge. You write graffiti
on the walls, cover stale windowpanes,

while the jukebox spins 78s, Patsy Cline,
five plays for a quarter. Chrome edges

have constantly reminded you of deviled words.
We live in regret for everyone we've loved.
The lovers hold out their hands, whispering for a dance
in the corner under the lime-yellow light bulb
as steam seeps and grooves.

The Alien Said *Yes*

to disco balls and audio waves
and shiny, happy people wearing
boots for late-night benders. Maybe
we clamor for more saxophone
since listening to our tongues
just benefits the devil.
This is to say: take good notes
before returning home.
At the library, he said *Amen* again
and again to books. We tend
to ruin things here when we borrow.
We wear wristbands to show we
belong to a hospital or a concert
outside at a ranch. The cashier at
Cracker Barrel, where breakfast is
all day, mentioned belonging.
Like places inside us living in celestial
space. Also, rings to show *commitment.*
Do you have this word? For the sweet
ever-loving. For who we're gone for.
Gravity is different. And those other
balls, *yes,* look like planets but
more like giant ice cream dots.
Strawberry. Lemon. Blueberry.
And the wall is the bottom curvature
of a tangerine cup you hold.
Let me show you. Take my hand.
Crash-landing in New Mexico
is rough if you want to ship

all that water back. Drought is yellow,
with a mouth that hardly speaks but
its speech has seen plenty of distance.
Remember to take note of one's
whole life. When we extinguish,
we leave behind dust clouds,
zigging in and out.

It's Come to This

I can't make you kiss the clouds
whispering over

the skin of the ocean. Looking away
from a sailboat shrinking—

a memory of our future
no longer buoying.

Not as flower stems that rest
in your lap, the tide of a gold

skirt. It's come to pass. Your white-laced
wings jut from red silk. Each silent

moment is a fabric. *Te amo*—
no matter. I fell from the cliff

nearby. I've come to
keep sight of you.

I Tried to Write a Memoir Called *Low Country Debacle;* I Failed

The way the pebble moon

fails to quiet the night's canopy. And sweetgrass isn't certain
      of the tide.

The way okra is chased down at the Piggly Wiggly,
      never finding their containers.

Now the gumbo's verb tense won't thicken

its voice. Just when my anxiety rises
      in little tents needing stakes for loose

sand. The way I realized doubt lowers
      my ability to drive a car

with air in the brake lines. Not knowing broke on
      bad luck, I was raised to believe I'd know

the answers. I don't. This is a test with bubbles I can't fill.

The way a woman once punctured my green balloon
      on St. Patrick's Day with her lit cigarette

or how, after airbags deploy, the sternum fractures.

Me? I'm marginal.

I keep writing in the margins instead. *The fragility of the body.*

I drank several margaritas splashed with Grand Marnier
       last night. Only Becca, the bartender, knows how.

It's an excellent way to end a chapter: cloudy.
       I drank gobs of water to prepare.

The other day, I wrote a self-portrait poem
       as consolation. The mirror conceit
had a zillion pieces. Lost. Glittering bits. Stars.

When I Dial Up the Elements of a Reggae, Rock, and Punk Band

Dabbing their T-shirts, The Rolling Stones
fed our dreams
hot blur

air quaffed in cannabis scented
from
someone like Angie from the song, a

jacketed bee since
her act
stung nothing
to no one

~~~

I'm fifteen in hormonal over-
flow, road-trip
Charlotte

struck on a school night, banks of coffee
and
No-Doz, the biology teacher drove

drumstick tapping
steering wheel
not stopping
for anyone

~~~

We sketched lyrics   brown paper
school hallway
banner

bootleg vinyl   scratched   bad stylus
the
cassettes stolen   from a zippered case

fuel to handle
living
zero else mattered   we translated don't care as *cara*
not better grades

~~~

Helen   winged-pretty prom date
Johns Island
address

embarrassed   my father drove us, she
sang
    from the front seat   my tongue throbbed in back

a buckskin Olds-
mobile
    catapulting on zilch   hopeless
lit red and alive

When the Whole World Wears a Costume

Late June night, on your living room floor,
each moment in a dinosaur outfit is not
a failure. The tasseled carpet talks cheap:
I'm the Captain of fun, honeybun.
You see the cliff marks of the present
dressed up as an ice cream globule—
all creamy, soft, and wavy. What hums?
The glow of bare lightbulbs slants
the lighting, buzzes the camped-out
horizon above the pizza slices.
The plants with spindly, dark vines
breathe what oxygen is here, behind
the TV, or beside the baby porcupine staring
from a striped cup as if puzzled, while
asking, "Why are you home this
often?" Here, a cup might house
your animal delight, weighing
down passages of ever-clear sanity
or did sanity take root twelve hundred
miles from here in Akron, Ohio, where
the backyard black cherry tree canopied
seven good years with you, smelling
tire-scented air and burnt leaves? Memory
doesn't voice how many miles anymore.
                        Open the future
behind you
            in a black drawer.

When Molecules Shed at the Driveway Movie Party

The night before Christmas, the crow arrives
to unload ribboned packages of breath.

Friends in portable chairs underneath the carport
don't notice due to its quiet, unassuming voice.

They ask if I need more Pinot Noir. Then we're glowing
silhouettes gazing at the white-linen screen

while watching *It's a Wonderful Life*. But when
I try blowing my nose in a Kleenex, I can't

unwrap its mini package fast enough. And the next
morning, I don't smell the pecan coffee

or taste the Vietnamese cinnamon.
When the clothes dryer buzzes, the crow says socks

do not need to match. They remain splayed on
the beige bathroom counter.

The crow lets the shower water run,
lets it jet my face

since I'm too miserable to move. He caws into
my lungs—a softness, his lullaby.

He makes me his song.

See Silver

We're in a museum. Sienna wooden

pedestal rests inside a showcase. A mouth

races open, a dark mini stove. We're

in Guanajuato, and currently on view is Juanito,

the smallest mummy. We stand in silence.

Eye the naked truth. We read captions.

See silver where we are mined in starlight.

A miner who cradles his son's face.

Blood vessels voice apologies. Now bones.

Scraps of yesteryear clothes. We hear dogs

later that night, where the unburied once rested,

barking off their neon collars under manicured

trees. Eye for a world on exhibit. Eye for Juanito's

arms folded as if to mind his mother on display

next to him. Tonight, the children outside

have no idea what ground they're dancing on.

They have the treasure of troubadour songs.

The children rest before the silent shattering.

Still-Life with Three Musicians and a Dog

He arrives after the parochial bells clanged, seeking a latte lavanda, but instead finds three musicians. One is black-masked

like a bandito. Another strums a guitar in an orange-and-yellow costume, and the third is a friar, black robed, holding sheet music.

He never finished the final sleep act. Lips hung over from last night's perfume at Sinatra's. He wanted a latte, not these colorful

musicians. Not to learn the café machine is broken and the lavender sprigs vanished. Never accept tea from a box of tea bags.

Select Earl Grey, perhaps steep two bags to calm. His mood is lopsided, sitting at a rickety table. Morning is a paper cutout,

held back by tasting latte lavanda. Instead, the clarinet arcs a song miraculously played by two hands but only one long, thin arm.

Cubed bold planes. A chocolate mocha dog hears in disbelief. Claws holding on. Same boxy brown stage. Why not try guitar

lessons again? It's time to steal an instrument. Rip beautiful notes. He wished for a latte lavanda. Steamed foam melody.

Now, he has a resolution.

Shelter

I gather kindling for light flecks, violet
flames for the future. Green branches never broke,
but cut ones, hinged open at the mouth, spoke.
Piney woods swallow breath. Breeze of the silent
gulf coast sways above red-brown dirt, turns violent.
Rest the voice of disdain. We know it pokes
to tame the body if it could. Rain wakes,
pierces the inevitable, burnt heart, an amulet.

Hands makeshift as a tent to protect
your camp. You cannot tie a canopy
over a big thicket wildfire. The toss
of trees snakes the hot and cold air, reflecting
in the mind, that swamp cooler commonly
breaks. What is the shelter for loss?

When Life Calmly Gives Out Its Secret

The hummingbird in a charcoal suit
buzzes the bush sage.

Fleeting moment. A fluttering melody.
Sun spikes the velvety light off Calle Loreto.

I sit behind the tiki blinds,
rhythm coming on.

I want to wear today like crepe
or vicuña fabric I'm not

supposed to wear. People vanish
like patterns on a blanket.

I need the shape of thirst. To save
those I love, I need a crowbar.

The Quiet Undoing

Night, July, in front of the spotlit tree, a possum rests
displaying her suit as if modeling on a runway.

No one is left to shoot the feral hogs. They multiply again, grazing
between the parking garage and the office complex.

Water gurgles from a broken water main
past the driveway deep enough to soak leather shoes.

The city has wrapped yellow caution tape around its slats.
I wish the sunken-in freeway refused

to become a river full of floating semi-tank trucks. I wish
the petrochemical plants would have their last disasters,

that hydrocarbon vapor would plume away, promenading
in a self-guided parade. But where to? Gulf redfish no longer

suit up. Jellyfish still sting, but I hope they don't mind
washing ashore a little more. At this point,

I want permission to talk to other living creatures.
I want focus groups, partners in crime.

Hummingbirds aren't suspects since they're too busy
in suspension, satisfying their turbo-charged metabolisms.

I can't believe we're just blips
with Mother Earth. I don't want to run away.

I wish the white jasmine wouldn't quiet. At the university,
no shriveling is allowed along the running trail.

Newspaper Photograph of Border Agents Discussing the Separation of a Family

Day wakes on a gravel road
                in front of flattened grass.
Four men and a woman,
                or maybe five men.
Guns holstered, thumbs hanging
      on belts from olive pants.
                Cargo pockets.

They stand, probably talking.

A little girl with a hazy purple dress
        clings to a leg, hiding her face.

This is not about a lost doll,
or walking in circles to win a cake,
        or flying a kite over June's roses.

This is about the slippery slope
                    of *zero tolerance*.

The headlines say so.

This is a place where cheap tickets get punched,

      where slipperiness travels on film.

Miracles do not live on the tongue.

Tapping fingers for answers is
    its melody.

Wait. In this new curbside reality, who is

the parent? Or agent?

Upon Seeing the Glorious Crepuscular Rays

If the end is coming, I want
to saddle up to cloud shadow
scattering the etched air, gazing
upon a field and the pines.

Cloud shadow milks the sky white.
Wavelength weighing on the landscape.
They sunbeam overtly and pour
into starkness.

Cloud shadow folding like a German
quilt, stitched brilliantly. The grand
artist wishes a pleasant twilight.
Gentleness comes.

Whispering wind whirls. If the end
is coming, enchant the Earth until
the finish line—a thin, yellow ribbon
that unfurls.

When the end arrives, no need
to forward the mail. Let the narrow
footpath weave like a ventricle
from the heart to siphon the ground.

Sky-broken lyrics.
Songs scratch the hills.
If the crows keep circling,
then eventually

they will caw. They yearn
for hunger. They eye
creatures below, especially
the lonely, lovely one.

I Will Talk Peace

Peace is not a dove carrying a freshly plucked olive leaf,
but I know love flies at first sight in a soup kitchen.

I leave my mark in New York
as the *Lady Bountiful of the Bowery.*

I am no angel. It helps to dispense food and medicine.
I shed pounds of fear off people

coerced by war. Our depressed affairs.
I will keep this place until everyone

has plenty. Everyone has pieces
of need, even the plants.

People who cannot see will have spectacles.
People who cannot walk will have wheelchairs.

Mother sends me images to sketch on scraps of paper.
A bird watches hypnotically.

White flower petals floating in dark water cool me.
Waves fleck in foam. My mystic passage.

I know the bird shadow orders my eyes closed to travel
behind the veil. Not to see any more planes and burning

buildings. The bird drinks in my hair.
Beyond the veil, I dream of white-blotched

clouds without smoke. The bird will whisper
my soul to heaven if I've done enough.

Peace is a letting go. I mist away
from black and white brushwork.

Peace is love on chapped lips.
A calm current. The talons and beaks
of the world will come for my flesh.

License Renewal

I hope no one is in line behind me—
this font is teeny. I must
read each line aloud as if it's a casino aglow.

I'm glad the vision test did not go below that line,
or I would have to leave again to get my eyes fixed,
and who knows how long that would take—certainly more
than the one-hour limit of this rescheduled appointment.

When I return with my forgotten Social Security card
and my passport after the taxi driver accepted my dicey
proposal to race home, I arrive with five minutes to spare.

An alien has not transformed me. No facial surgery
has occurred; no instruments are left inside my body.

I admit my personality has changed.
I'm more in love with feta cheese-filled olives.
Lemons are a summer non-starter, but now
I love wearing my lemon-patterned shirt.

By coming to the DMV today, I admit that my tongue,
hidden in the newly required photo, is worn
to a pulp. Now I add hot sauce.

I admit my mouth opens too much, and I will try
to shut it more frequently in the future. I promise to drive
more carefully despite having no points. I'm going to harness

every muscle in my patient heart when others drive that Russian
roulette speed in a non-school zone. I'm still on Earth banking
to stay in my lane. I will try not to activate someone's rage

or mine. I admit there's no fire extinguisher for my personality's
various components. Please accept this application. Therefore,
I am ready to sign. Please help me see where.

Reunion

We getaway and wait where golden eagles soar over grassland. Burrow holes punch in dirt patches. We return to the historical marker north of Marathon and unfold lawn chairs at the edge of a ranch road. We crack tabs on morning Lone Stars, ready to lounge again for hours to see what flies by but not to drink too much, to tap down greed for a lucky flyover. We stop sipping when a dark wingspan unzips the horizon. A cunning, suitcase heart.

Each time I hold breath
a seam appears from a sunspot.
The breathing poets
unpack words at the casita,
dream of rocks to break
them open.

Letter to Lincoln Fox

Dear Lincoln: It's fitting to see your statue, *Dream of Flight,* upon landing at the Albuquerque airport. I think about being *free from the confines of the earth's surface* when I start snapping pictures of clouds from the airplane window. You were probably not thinking of ascending to the crest of the Sandias via the aerial tramway, but it doesn't matter. My *imagination's free to receive greater truths* in the panoramic view, the gin & tonics at the elevated bar, and the walk near the ski lift. I'm still deciding if the bronze six-pack abs apply. I don't know if the loincloth and fancy cap are supposed to lift off as one foot touches a handful of rocks. I'm open to the possibility that a spiritual bird with a large wingspan would accept my right-handed grip—although I'm left-handed—as well as the other bird, perhaps a dove, resting on my noggin as if to navigate a direction. *Closed thinking and poverty of spirit* require effort to overcome. I'm fluttering north to soak my skin and molt in the Ojo Caliente pools. I received the massage therapist's urge to take the scrub brushes home. I accept the sweat wrap, hoping someone remembers to unwrap me so I can breathe again. Fear keeps my eyes below—where, you won't say—maybe under a piñon tree, and fear keeps my eyes split open despite the dry air. And now I must claim my baggage at the carousel. I'm looking forward to the adventure. I didn't realize that until now.

The Whole World Is a Work of Art

In the moment of undoing, I crumble

      guapa   for flamenco dancers.

Old theater   a *biblioteca* seat for 300 pesos.

      Murals. Scarf from a passed-away friend.

Dance as if to break.   I'm a chair she curves around.

The calcium woven into cavities.

A knife lit with gunpowder cauterizes

an arrow wound   a scene from *Two Mules for Sister Sara*.

She's a strong-willed nun but she's not.   It's none of that

bliss creek. I'm a train.   She is dynamite. Lodged in bridge

trestles   a fantasy shot   shooter's eye sparks the bullet.

Walk to the post office for *Forever* stamps,

piñata pictures tasseled stars and saddled donkeys

    confetti-speckled sky ready for a God   blindfolded

to whack apart   hard-candied stomachs.

My legs   guitar strings strung

to hobble home. Lemon morning. This gallery is a dance theater.

I'm a wood dragon   breath ablaze   burning ships.

Climbing Up to *Tres Cruces,*
San Miguel de Allende

I even love the alarm of dogs after Three Kings Day,
their barks behind a purple-tinseled fence. I
was smiling up this mountain in honey-dropped
late afternoon, after crossing jeopardy highway,
and the earlier plunge, mining a tamarind slush pile,
torched orange peel menued as a margarita;
still smiling at the climb ahead.
Crosses erase evil spirits, pivoting
around a shaft inside, grounded with sprawls of gold.
Last year, endurance bit deep.
Red-and-white antennas, purveyors in candy cane bodies,
fastened and hushed over the poet's memorial stone.
R.C. loved this hike every January to have
a better lick of heaven.

Afterward, we mourners sip clear tequila,
slug punches of citrus and spice. Wood
and bougainvillea crowd a patio of straw donkeys
at Starbucks. I need to catch up on blurriness.
So much searching, I hardly know where
to start. Don't look back and become skin and bone.

Cooking Class

Instead of watching the cooking channel in bed,
we watched Big Joe cook it live across the street.
Under low heat and overhead mirrors, betting
on ratios of pyramids. *How much of the Trinity is celery,
onion, and green pepper?* Sacrifices of little bodies
as if warriors fighting evil spirits. Wrists bent
with knives. Cutting board on a stone
counter, the tiny green hands of cilantro,
basil as dogwood's twin, the interior hulls
of seeds, animal pieces feeding our souls.
How did the fish get so far inland? Stirring roux
is climbing stairs. We learned about flux,
energy as a slow burn. *Do not use straight water.*
If our tongues want to dance, let's find
a ballroom. We know cooking isn't our forte—
that wasn't the point; the heat is in breaking open.

Comfort

Now that I've found a masseuse, I splurge on mellow comfort
inside a house off Shepherd. Hot rocks converge, yellow comfort.

Enjoying a more aligned back, I sail waves of sheets. Buoy nights
on a mattress near drywall.
                  A mouse gnaws, unnerved, glowing comfort.

Over and over, before people leave, they aim rifles at my stars,
falling flat. People swell like weather,
                  submerging climate, slowing comfort.

Baggage carried the worst contents to the curb of history—
boomerang breakups and crinkled wound bandages.
It's disturbing, hard-to-swallow comfort.

And loaded atop my baggage—blood swipes, memory thumb
drives, and bullets in coin envelopes—crests of magical
thinking to purge, far below comfort.

Technically, time in the past doesn't exist. I need to
clean the closet and donate carloads of clothes.
Willows for strangers, merging the pillowed comfort.

Invitation

John, no need to worry.
A piece of bread is only
a piece of bread.
John, keep it if you want
or give one or two pieces to your guests
or not.
You do not have to count.
No fair share because betrayal is eating supper.

If you want to offer a gentle touch to Mary
wrapped in her red-and-olive cloth.
If you want to drink more wine,
just ask for more, no need to keep glasses full.

And no need to cut the roasted lamb
in the turquoise bowl. You have never
liked fava beans, so do not eat those.
Or the lettuce heads.

Be gentle on yourself, looking holy
with a halo. A moon sliver awaits
your naked body behind these brown panels.
John, it's the last night to dance.
So go, laugh, and say,
"I will. Yes, I will."

Born to Be Wild

Believe in the wild before wildness.
Speak from a boat. Speak when nudity
sees foliage dress the shoreline
with a dark hem. Speak for her, elbows
raised, hands wedged behind the head.
Speak for tranquility, that surface speaks
for adventure from a faintly tinted, red face.
Believe in wild as a magic carpet ride,
flying over sparrows, once a band
who sang from a Canadian village
buttoned with orchards and cider houses.
Believe in gods who say you don't
have to celebrate clothing anymore.
You don't have to celebrate what's in
the closet. How to imagine bare skin
is how to touch someone.
He is seeking. Or seems lost. Or he
is deciding where to land, believing
lessons from epic trips that failed.
Believe in running with the current,
coming whatever way and feeling
nature's coolness as if drinking
a truth serum. As if contemplation
is a country. As if wind carries time.
Believe in the wild before boarding
the boat to cast off tired stories
from before. Forget past losses,
happy endings, love's embrace.
Whether he will return
is hard to know.

Blood & Air

When the guitar riffs elevate
on U2's "Song for Someone,"
it's like driving home from work,
and I admit to stealing away time
at 4:45 p.m. before anyone knew
I left via the secret stairwell, except
security at the front desk
who doesn't care but says
"have a good evening"
to my horse-monogrammed blue shirt,
and wrinkle-free khakis after exiting
a parking garage in Houston's
energy corridor—like trying to unsheathe
enough wire to solder a complete circuit
to play this song of direction.
I can almost hear the lead and tin melt
its way ahead, so my ears can let loose
despite the seatbelt. And just like that,
I'm all grown up with one eye open
in twilight for someone I loved who was not
home. I'm not a genius. I run between
the hedges of the whole world in a dark
suit. I stole a kiss from your mouth
while standing in a fog on an offshore rock.
As if to rekindle our conversation. As if
your starlit silhouette drives in, and I drive
in despite my back that can't take the soft earth.
I need a mattress. I'm resigned as a seed to
the wind. A root will begin again in melody.
When the first bud opens, I know you will sing
its scent.

When Are We Arriving?

You walk her obnoxious dog
down Southgate in the August
sauna while wearing church
clothes only to realize love is
a chore. And you're better off
buying stargazers instead of roses,
forgetting to lose yourself
in a lover's gaze—might as well chain
your corduroys to the bedframe.
Hardly a 1,001 Arabian night scene.
On Earth, every romance is a boat ride.
How else to describe all the unexpected
Waves, the brine, the floundering
against riptides, the unexpected strokes,
another Sunday not going to church,
instead praying inside a spice store
for a gratis jar of garlic? We're all trying
to unscrew lids for crumbles of joy
to roll on our tongues, coarse or fine.
We laugh, coarse or fine.
In Houston, summer is not an outdoor activity.
Stupidly, I miss the steam.
Still, like you, I speak into clouds bruised
and pleading, and besides serving you
breakfast in bed, I'll move your furniture.
I'll walk your dog again if you want me to.

Driving to Dallas on Good Friday
for My Brother's Oyster Roast

Trace the boring segment
of I-45, again, as if in pencil lead,
its tip will inevitably break
into a smattering of pieces.

Indian paintbrush squeeze,
bend in costume along the shoulder
of steeped grass before Buffalo,
wavelengths of air curve.

The bug-splattered windshield.
Gasoline burns off a violet vapor.
The Fairfield picnic unwraps
on an iron table behind Mickey D's.

The Easter lily and beer passengers
need the bathroom break, a stall inside
the Corsicana Outlet Mall, passing
the Accurate Weight Scale and *Dubble Bubble*

gumball machine standing like sentries, no qualms
guarding a darkened, empty store I once loved
for marked-down socks and blue jeans. Blocks
away from my brother's house, I offer to buy

chunks of mesquite. Notice a bronze couple,
life-sized figurines, pushing a giant, stainless steel egg
towards a straw nest in an apartment complex.

Park across the street at the destination.
In the guest room chair, convince the luggage to play
trapeze. Downstairs, on the kitchen counter, mix
a concoction. Horseradish. Cocktail sauce. Lime. To parcel

in tiny silver cups. A white golden retriever,
chin-planted on the patio, manages
the grill's behavior, its radiant
black dome. Knife at seams after charcoal

steams the oval tombs. Unhinge joy,
to caress our tongues with salt and zinc.

Cento: What Kind of Quagmire Is This?

incorporating lines from Ada Limón and Tony Hoagland

The place where the sky is white
        with June's teeth. Air is ash and woodsmoke.
A river oak knows we were conned for something.
        It is when your intimacy coordinator's mouth presses
against your ear, thicker now, the summer muck,
        her lips lean out of the same sky, white.

It is the feeling within. How your creaking body,
        empty, isn't jump-started by your fight director.
You can take pain relievers, read,
        and swim, water under you so deep.

It is touching a calm flag of surrender pulled taut
        by afternoon. It is trying to take
the lima bean from a baby's mouth. You are rejected.
        Misfortune.

It is when a lawyer stands beside your car,
        removes sunglasses, looks up at the sky,
marries you, claims a clean slate of secrets,
        and knows how to carry you.

A flush of color from a dying tree doesn't help. Neither does
        aspirin nor cocaine. A bucket full of lawyer jokes
can't make you laugh.
        Injustice.

It is drab grass, watching a dog suffer heat stroke,
        and you, weeping. That moment when you step away
from the party after looking for what's left.
        Darkness is a big, beautiful face.

It is when images appear distorted in suburbia,
        and you aren't large from this distance.
It's Houston. Any leaves this month tuck themselves into the gulf.
        Any time the warm breast of a dental hygienist,

who leans to access your plaque, is available, you realize
        you're having a winner-dinner
dream with your mother.

No. You are not speeding through this barrel-round
        belly of a summer. Cooler days have leaked
from your memory, fed down a feeder road. No U-turn,
        all gullet.

Home Run

My son, who doesn't exist, enters the baseball stadium
wearing an orange cap embedded with rhinestones. He sits

in the nosebleed section, shelled peanuts in a clear zip-lock
bag. I'm horrified. He is allergic to bees, the first sting years

before in his grandmother's small-town backyard after tagging
first base, the trunk of a nameless blossoming apple tree.

*

After playing catch with my father in the alley, I never passed
down the glove. I'll never hear my son yell *Hey, Harry!*

to the White Sox broadcaster who cantilevered a fish net
from a booth to catch foul balls. I wish my son liked the drizzle

of melted butter, layered for popcorn, from a Teflon-flecked
saucepan. I wish he had won pennants.

*

How do you swing at joy and run to taste its outcome?
How do you touch someone and know whether you're in reach?

I'm not Captain Imagine. Go on, climb the apple tree. Eat the pie.
My hands hang your bright jersey in the cedar closet.

Pasture

Tuesday morning is murder. The intersection is holy knotted,
breakfast tacos foiled out there, waiting in suburbia,

aware their rosy cheeks want our kisses, but now you;
you're knifing at our hunger and ETAs. Your exoskeleton

body inserts into Shepherd—the street needs car shepherds,
room to roam, and you pretend crumpled, orange road cones

are burrs in your fleece. We wish grey wolves would bite your
neck. We here must appear as sheep in a pasture

perpendicular, yet still trapped by your blockade. No,
we goats stagger to this star-bursted

abyss hoping for disgruntled roughage, wanting to sleep
on raised platforms, pallets, to dry away our urine,

directionally above you, near the nude house begging
to sell, its yellow signs say no credit check. Do you think we're

kidding when we say our snouts can sense your spine? As humans,
we're blood-signed a scroll saying we'll find tenderness

in every living creature except now, because of you,
we'll reconvene our congress

to amend. With our four-compartment stomachs,
truth digests. We will horn this rudeness out.

Epiphany

It's like that encounter,
hair shampoo forgotten,
junk in the grocery cart,
Saturday dusk after
last night's bust,
recovering the car
from a disco parking lot,
half-bloodshot eyes,
a bag of potato chips
in hand, here
you meet any ex-lover
who thinks they knew
you then, all your pasts
tucked in the aisles
of savory or sweet.

Aging Disgracefully

Arthritis sends apologies, brittle cottonwood.
Before the undoing, call to be picked up. I can't
don a face of
embarrassment in
front of my brother.
Good. Along White Rock Lake,
hope is praying for just a muscle pull.
Indigo is a coat wearing wisdom,
jubilant isolation—its love,
kindness driving me to the sports doctor.
Luminous stapled pages depict exercises at home—
many stretches for hips & legs, pelvic tilts, cat-cows, you
name it, described inside the pockets of a blue folder,
obviously ready for heaps of
patients who are seen daily, knowing
quality of living has drifted to a screened-in porch,
recliner nearby that doesn't ask questions. Doesn't
squash words like a runover honeydew.
The music cues on a rubber band, the worst C&W,
underscoring the walk. A windblast. A giant swamp drain.
Varieties of wild hibiscus await and afar.
Whatever. The right hamstring hoists a sail of agony.
X-rays confirm later an eerie white glow.
Yesterday, that god,
Zephyr, passed by, a lyrical breeze, done & gone.

Shocking Love Poem

I was scaling the inside
of a snuff bottle when a
washed-up genie whispered
my lover reported me
missing. Whatever—
familiar, wishful
rubbing for a wish you
didn't expect. You get what
you give. So, I laced up
my shoes, ignoring the tobacco
aroma and sharpened
my eye to race laps on a jade
track. Running to flatten
my figure for escape, so I
can pursue my dream of
training with kangaroos
(they appreciate me)
who store energy in tendons
like a spring leaping over
crackling wires again and again
unfazed.

If Life Is So Much More Evaluating Than It Appears, Why Isn't There a Hotline to Call?

If I could make it out of here alive, I'd take
the emergency *go* bag. Sure, this works against

a celestial path, but I am complex. I want ninety days
in rehab to wean off my life's obsessions. Like media

absorption, for instance, solving word puzzles and eating
bacon and tomato sandwiches. I want a pair of well-made

shoes, a screened-in porch, and a cozy chair to comfort
the achy organs. I was born in slowness; it only

worsened as it sped up. In my suburban corner office, my boss
says *slow down* to self-check work. As if time is allowed to

dance in a mad flamenco I can't miss. And here I am, the last
one left in the theater, clapping my hands at the empty chairs.

The Dodo

You say these birds
went extinct after the boots
I'm wearing were made,
meaning dodo birds smelled
boots like these before—
              time expires fast.
The untamed ostrich
approaches for feed pellets
              divebombing
the bag in my lap
once I opened a window.
My life flamed—
              no chance
for making babies.
When we tail ourselves out
of this discounted wildlife park,
we lace our fingers to form
a chapel.
              What is
the flight of our scent?

One Night I Pretended the World Didn't Exist

The shadowy night she rejected me,
I saw a yellow-crowned night heron, dead.

The heron lay on the brick esplanade,
honeycombed bile, a vein trickling in grass blades.

A troupe of horseflies circled, tricking the buttery
lamp glow, a trapeze act swinging from live oaks.

When you're living on romance wings,
you love a feather after sipping red wine

at The Tasting Room. Some days, you wind up
sprouting a beautiful self, a theater door

in a glass wall. I can't find the doorway.
Someday, I will escape the nightshade.

What Gentles Skin But Isn't

Always walking at night, then self-talk, "working the path, detour from danger on the walk," walking past the mysterious joy house, hearing the waterfall trickle and the speckled cat guarding the driveway, a meditation too brief when strolling along Vassar, walking to the next block, often stopping for the rest stop of an egret sipping from a puddle, striding over to the other sidewalk, talking "not the plan, accept the divine surprise;" often on edge with the iffy rain; often the accidental trip off an uneven sidewalk which is not a disaster assuming not a face fall, lying for hours on end with a concussion or worse, lost consciousness, which isn't 100% disastrous since this affluent neighborhood—the other side of the freeway—would call an ambulance even this late; often selecting the walking route and hoping for five gold stars; often remembering who walked to protest a salt tax, which wasn't a walk but a *march* against heavy salt tax; often the best walks lead to arrest, lambasting the heaviest acts of rule; often stopping to see nests in the live oaks with midnight wondering about their vacancies, and the dark air as media to fluff and permeate a body, to filter tomorrow morning's light, while mumbling "rejoice at the moonlit heaven and energy which gentles the skin but isn't!"

Aubade with Circle Game

Begin by contemplating a dot,
then reflect on a line wiggling

as a sparkling redfish that spirals close to
a dark blue boat drawn off the coast, beaches

with plenty of compact sand, thrown perfectly,
an auburn frisbee feeling like vinyl, an LP ready

to needle the future, then gulf fallen,
but recovered by your lover's hand

when the sky was full
of high cloudlets. Despite the sloppy

throws and blisters, you keep throwing
and catching.

*

I'll eventually love August, days dripping by.
And the seasons they go round and round.

The frontier of a small radio, jostling
the antenna to work—clothes as a costume—

cartwheels thru the town. Round with decent
looks, and later, we escape the escape room

masquerading as art, we press fingertips on.
Lights dot up lines under a starry night to

reveal clues that help secure
the Declaration of Independence and unscramble

wooden blocks to spell: *teamwork.*
A hidden door unlocks.

We can't return, we can only look. Yes, I
love kissing farewell to old, traditional paint,

monsters left inside at palace altars. Dear, let us
throw our gentle bodies into the swamp. Peat

forms coal, fuel for the simple gesture of joining
together, sheets of someday, the pristine circle.

Willy Wonka

You've never seen a silver museum in Texas.
You don a grey wig with a bald cap
in the office bathroom stall. For your acting
role of a geezer who begins to dance
allegro, deflecting co-workers'
normally dagger-eyed. Now, they hover around
your blueberry chairs. As if this new
assignment is a golden ticket. You
portray Grandpa Joe, measuring steps
in over-the-moon ecstasy up the parking deck,
faking the need for handrails to the top ramp
despite the spring swelter. The chili cookoff's
Chili Wonka. You are a turtle in a woolen
shell, pajama skin underneath,
crawling in a concrete habitat. It's better
to laugh at other co-stars than watch
seniority bake. No one needs to know who
you are, so pretend you're Jack Albertson.
One hand to help stir the pot,
but not ask why there are no beans.
The other hand holds a cane you don't
need. One that won't save your tongue
from radioactive heat, causing your taste buds
to escape. You find a secret camp
where cowboys squat around a fire,
swapping stories about wild ponies
over plain saltines. Somehow, *thrill*
sounds like a grown-up word for
salvation. Somehow, *allegro* must
measure happiness on the world
spin-o-meter, where you cannot

see the needle. And now you realize:
joy is a good egg—the world hasn't
thrown you down a garbage chute. Yet.
Now you learn who survives fantasyland.
Who rides a glass elevator, who finds
their way to the ground.

When the Whole World Is Short-Staffed

You find it in someone's voice
occasionally—those softened echoes
of kindness, precious bits, pearl or silver.
It's before the world went off
and made a mask for itself, persistently
short-staffed, announcing in a faded
display sign on the crowned surface
of a hostess stand. These days,
kindness sleeps on the street
and lights a bad wick. It defies
the downtrodden and carries rechargeable
batteries. Kindness doesn't care that I
possess a stupid heart. Inside the restaurant,
ravens, lamplight, shadows splash. Kindness
has a waiter who isn't here to greet us,
to give out crayons to draw the evening
on brown paper. I love kindness's vacancies,
the motel of it creeping along the roadside.
Its coupons rested in a late-night diner rack,
its glass door holding back a wild wind draft.
On New Year's Eve, after the champagne splurge,
kindness is empty, and everyone's outside
staring at the stars. Burning wood chunks in an urn,
confetti dressing the trees. I douse embers
with water, then watch from my warm home.
Thank you. I'm calm now, cat
clawing upstairs, climbing under bed covers,
the gentle silk of kindness's exit, light glowing
red out of my window. I fall asleep.

Notes

"Prayer Is a Vast Country" is based on Francisco Antonio Vallejo's painting, *Christ After the Flagellation*.

The title, "The Man Who Fell to Earth," is borrowed from a 1976 film starring David Bowie. The poem is inspired by James Cochran's painting, *Bowie Wall, Brixton, London*.

"Pissarro" is after Pissarro's painting, *Boulevard Montmartre at Night*.

"When the Whole World Wears a Costume" is after Daphna Kato's painting, *Snack*.

"Born to Be Wild" is after Alexander Harrison's painting, *Solitude*.

"It's Come to This" is after Antônio Rafael Pinto Bandeira's painting, *Young Woman Seated*.

"You Can't Always Get What You Want" is loosely based upon Carlos Verger Fioretti's painting, *Phalaena*.

The title of "Still-Life with Three Musicians and a Dog" is after Pablo Picasso's painting of the same title.

"I Will Talk Peace" is after Marian Spore Bush's painting, *Peace*.

The italicized words in "Aubade with Circle Game" come from Joni Mitchell's song, *The Circle Game*.

"Upon Seeing the Glorious Crepuscular Rays" is after Katja Lang's painting, *Cloud Shadows*.

"Invitation" is after Sister Plautilla Nelle's painting, *The Last Supper*.

Rilke inspired me to write "When Life Calmly Gives Out Its Secret."

About the Author

John Milkereit resides in Houston, Texas, working as a mechanical engineer and has completed an MFA in Creative Writing at the Rainier Writing Workshop. His work has appeared in various literary journals, including *The Orchards Poetry Journal, The Comstock Review, Panoply,* and *The Ekphrastic Review.* He has published two chapbooks (Pudding House Press) and four full-length collections of poems, including *Lost Sonnets for My Unvaccinated Lover* (Kelsay Books, 2023).

www.ingramcontent.com/pod-product-compliance
Lightning Source LLC
Chambersburg PA
CBHW022015160426
43197CB00007B/446